Written by Mary Boone

Hilary Duff

Total Hilary, Metamorphosis, Lizzie McGuire and More!

TRIUMPH
ENTERTAINMENT
Division of Triumph Books
601 South LaSalle Street
Chicago, Illinois 60605

over Photo by Robert Mora/Getty Images • This Page Photo by Evan Agostini/Getty Images

CONTENTS

THE EARLY DAYS:
How Hilary Became a Star

becoming Lizzie McGuire

Big Screen Dreams

FANS LOVE HILARY

making a difference

Publisher
Bob Baker • Bailey Park Consulting

Written by
Mary Boone

Art Direction
Michael Stassus • Rockett Media

About the Author
This is author Mary Boone's third book for children and young adults. She also has written for magazines including *People*, *Teen People*, *Mary-Kate and Ashley*, and *Entertainment Weekly*. Mary lives in Tacoma, Wash., with her husband, Mitch Robinson, and their two children, Eve and Eli.

About the Designer
Michael Stassus has been editing and desiging publications for teens and young adults for ages. He served as Creative Director for *Teen Style*, *Electronic Gaming Monthly*, *The Official U.S. PlayStation Magazine*, and recently art directed the Official *Dr. Seuss' Cat in the Hat Behind-The-Scenes Movie Book* for Triumph and Universal Studios. Michael lives in the Chicago suburbs with his wife Sarah, and two daughters, Jillian and Lindsay.

TRIUMPH
ENTERTAINMENT
Division of Triumph Books
601 South LaSalle Street
Chicago, Illinois 60605

Road to Success

4

THE EARLY DAYS:
How Hilary Became a Star

While other teens are busy worrying about pop quizzes and homecoming dances, Hilary Duff spends her days memorizing movie scripts, signing autographs, and preparing for photo shoots. No doubt about it, the bubbly, blonde pop star is on top of the world.

People who don't recognize Hilary's name or sparkly eyes haven't seen TV, walked past a newsstand, listened to the radio, or been to a movie lately. She's everywhere these days:

• Hilary won a 2003 Nickelodeon Kids' Choice award for Favorite TV Show for her Disney Channel series Lizzie McGuire.

• When The Lizzie McGuire movie opened in May 2003, it was number two at the box office – topped only by mega hit X2: X-Men United.

• Metamorphosis, her first full-length solo album, was released in August 2003 and sold 204,000 copies its first week. Her bubbly tune So Yesterday claimed the top spot on Billboard's Hot 100 Singles Sales Charts.

• The WB celebrated her 16th birthday in September 2003 with a one-hour musical party taped in Hawaii.

• She's hauling in big bucks for film projects. In fact, she reportedly was paid $2 million to star in the upcoming A Cinderella Story.

• Her own line of clothing, shoes, cosmetics, jewelry, and dolls is due on store shelves by spring 2004.

But it hasn't always been like this. Hilary's childhood was pretty typical. Her parents, Bob and Susan Duff, and then two-year-old sister Haylie welcomed her into the world on September 28, 1987. The chubby-cheeked baby girl had a great demeanor from the start. She rarely cried and, even as an infant, she seemed amused by her big sis.

A true Libra, Hilary's wit and fashion sense were obvious when she was just a toddler. As a 3-year-old, she bugged her mom to let her wear red shoes everyday. "They went with everything – in her mind," mom Susan told People magazine.

As soon as she could walk, Hilary joined Haylie in performing around their suburban Houston home. The girls loved to dress up and do skits. They routinely sang and danced for their parents, neighbors, and whoever else would watch.

"Ever since I was 5, my sister and I used to watch TV and then we'd turn it off and act out the scenes together," Hilary told Your Magazine. "Haylie would say, 'Since you have short hair and I have long, pretty hair, you have to be the boy.' She was evil!"

The sisters were – and continue to be – inseparable. As young girls, they loved to play tag, hide and seek, and jump rope. These days the two are shopping maniacs. Hilary told TRL she admires the styles of stars like J Lo and Britney, but she gets most of her fashion and beauty hints from Haylie.

When she was 8, big sister Haylie talked her parents into letting her take ballet lessons. Not wanting to be left out, Hilary pleaded to start dance classes, too. The sisters loved ballet and their teachers saw promise in their not-quite-perfect plies and pirouettes. When she was 6, Hilary made her stage debut in Texas's BalletMet Columbus production of The Nutcracker.

To say Hilary and Haylie "liked" performing would be an understatement. They loved it! Soon the girls began attending a performing arts school in San Antonio.

"We started getting involved in school plays and singing," Hilary told AGirlsWorld.com. "My sister was doing a Romeo and Juliet Shakespeare play and there was a little acting workshop near our house. She started to go and my mom asked me if I wanted to go. I thought 'Oh no, that's so stupid. I would never want to do that.' But I just kind of followed in her footsteps."

By the time Hilary was 7 years old, the girls were enrolled in acting classes, modeling, auditioning for commercials, and hoping for success. Haylie got a bit part in the made-for-TV movie Hope. Not too long after that, Hilary got her first part in a local commercial. Then, in 1997, she got a small role in True Women, a mini-series being filmed in Texas. The TV movie starred Dana Delaney and Rachel Leigh Cook as friends who are separated as

Hilary and sister Haylie arrive at the opening of the Stella McCartney store this fall in Beverly Hills, California. The store is a high-end fashion store that caters to the Hollywood elite.

teens. Hilary's part was so small that her name didn't appear in the credits . . . still, it was a starting point.

Soon the Duffs realized if the girls were going to strike it big, they'd need to move to Los Angeles. So, mom, Hils, and Haylie – packed up and moved to California. The girls' dad stayed behind to run the family's chain of convenience stores in Texas. He still lives in Houston and travels to Los Angeles every three weeks or so to see the family.

The move west, remembers Susan Duff, was because of Haylie's desire to act. "Hilary kind of was dragged along. You know, whatever the big sister was doing, the little one wanted to do," Susan told MSNBC.

In the beginning, Haylie worked more than Hilary, so the younger sister tagged along on auditions and jobs. At first Hilary just sat on the sidelines, but soon she grew to love acting as much as Haylie – maybe even more.

Hilary always is quick to point out that her parents never pushed their daughters into acting.

"It was -- I wouldn't say my decision – I would say Haylie's decision," Hilary told MSNBC in September 2003. "I didn't really want anything to do with it and then we started modeling and getting involved in commercials and I fell in love with it too."

The Duff girls knew what they wanted to do, but getting jobs wasn't as easy as they had hoped it would be.

Hilary eventually got some commercial work and guest roles on television shows.

"We actually found a

manager in Texas who said, 'Give me $1,000 and I'll take you out to Los Angeles and I'll have all these auditions for you,'" Hilary told Fox News. "So, of course, we did that and she ditched us as soon as we got out there."

Refusing to give up, Susan Duff headed to the bookstore and bought every book she could find about getting started in show business, show business law, and how to get an agent. She learned about auditions, portfolios, and pilot seasons. (Pilot seasons are when networks produce a couple of episodes of new shows to see if audiences will like them. Successful shows become a regular part of the TV line-up. Dud shows are discontinued after an episode or two; sometimes they don't even make it on the air.)

The first pilot season came and went without much to show for it, but the Duffs were still hopeful.

Photo Courtesy Everett Collection

It took years of meetings and auditions for Hilary to get a handful of tiny parts. She was an extra on Chicago Hope and the girls worked on a pilot called The Underworld that Hilary – then 9 - barely remembers.

"The alien came through the window and ate us," Haylie told Rolling Stone, reminding her sister about The Underworld's plot.

The girls were about to call it quits and head back to the Lone Star State when Hilary landed the role of Wendy in 1998's "Casper Meets Wendy."

The movie, featuring actors George Hamilton, Cathy Moriarty, Shelley Duvall, and Teri Garr, tells the story of Desmond the Evil Warlock who wants to destroy Wendy the Good Little Witch. Even though Casper and Wendy are told that ghosts and witches just don't get along, the two become friends and prevent a supernatural showdown between their feuding families.

The direct-to-video follow-up to the 1995 movie Casper wasn't exactly a huge hit, but it got Hilary noticed. Film critic Richard Scheib wrote: "Hilary Duff has a certain sparkle as Wendy." And Needcoffee.com reviewers said: "Duff as Wendy . . . succeeds in being cute . . . it's hard to ask for more than that from a 10-year-old, even in a starring role."

Most importantly, it got her noticed by casting directors.

In 2000, it looked as if Hilary was on the verge of stardom. She was cast as one of the daughters in the NBC comedy Daddio, a show about a restaurant supply salesman who decides to leave his job and stay home to raise his family while his attorney wife goes back to work.

"I had been on so many auditions and I finally got it. I was really excited," Hilary told Fox Network's The Pulse.

Unfortunately, before Daddio ever aired, Hilary was dropped from the show. "I was like 'Oh my gosh' and I told my mom 'I want to go back to Texas' and she's like 'sure,'" Hilary remembers.

It was a real low point for Hilary, but her mom urged her to keep trying – and it's a good thing she did. A week later, she won the title role on the Disney Channel's Lizzie McGuire. And the rest, as they say, is history. ♥

Hilary makes an instore appearance at Toys "R" Us Times Square to promote Hasbro's VideoNow portable video player.

Photo by
Evan Agostini/Getty Images

becoming Lizzie McGuire

Hilary really didn't want to go to the Lizzie McGuire audition – in fact, she almost canceled it. Thank goodness she didn't.

After her first audition and two weeks of callbacks, Hilary got the part and the Lizzie McGuire legend began.

Soon Hilary gained world-wide recognition as the star of the Disney Channel's hit series. As Lizzie McGuire, she portrays (the series lives on in reruns) a charmingly klutzy teen-age girl

"Lizzie is a cool girl, but she is not always popular. I think people relate to her because maybe they are going through some of that too."

The show, which began airing in 2001, quickly became the Disney Channel's top-rated sitcom and the No. 1 show on basic cable for girls ages 9 to 14. Eight Lizzie McGuire books have been published, and a full line of Lizzie McGuire apparel and accessories soon will be available nationwide.

Hilary thinks Lizzie's insecurities are the key to her popularity. "People relate to the show," she told The New York Times Upfront. "Every 14- or 15-year-old girl goes through the hard times at school and the embarrassing moments with their parents and the annoying little brother they just want to kill."

navigating middle school's rocky waters. She handles cliques, trendy styles, and boyfriends while her sassy animated alter ego provides commentary.

"Lizzie is a cool girl, but she is not always popular. She doesn't have a big group of friends and she is kind of awkward and she

doesn't really know who she is. I think people relate to her because maybe they are going through some of that too," she said

Hilary says the Lizzie role fit her perfectly. "It all seemed to come naturally," she told The Toronto Sun. "Half the time I didn't even know I was acting."

Disney Channel executive Gary Marsh told The Detroit Free Press that Hilary and Lizzie are very much alike

"She's adorable, No. 1," he said. "She's a smart kid and she's close enough to her character that Lizzie McGuire is an extension of her. She has more confidence than Lizzie

Seeing herself animated is odd, bu
to "Lizzie the Cartoon" tha

McGuire, and that's grown over the years."

Seeing herself as an animated character is odd, but Hilary says she often relates more to "Lizzie the Cartoon" than she does "Lizzie the Girl."

"My cartoon character is a little more edgy and snappy," she told Timeforkids.com.

"I love Lizzie McGuire. That's my character. That's my girl," Lizzie told Nancy O'Dell of Access Hollywood. "What was really cool about the show is that everyone goes through that stage of life feeling uncomfortable with themselves and not really knowing who they are, trying to fit in, trying to find out who you want to be, where you want to be."

While tweens and teens account for the largest group of Lizzie McGuire fans, the character's appeal doesn't end there. Parents, grandparents, and even celebrities such as Aerosmith rocker Steven Tyler, Saturday Night Live's Jimmy Fallon, and CBS newswoman Hannah Storm are fans of the show.

"I've had college students come up to me and say 'Oh my God, we love your show and our dorm doesn't have it, so we come home and at night we go to the next dorm to watch it,' which is really cool," Hilary told Fox News in May 2003.

As popular as Lizzie McGuire is, new shows are no longer being taped. In May 2003, Hilary decided to

Hilary says she often relates more he does "Lizzie the Girl."

"It's funny because I never, like, broke away. It wasn't like I'm leaving, I'm gone, I'm done. It was never like that."

walk away from the role altogether.

According to the Los Angeles Times, Disney wanted to move Lizzie from a junior high student on the Disney Channel to a blossoming high schooler in an ABC series. The studio reportedly was willing to raise Hilary's paycheck from $15,000 to $35,000 per

episode but her family was asking $100,000.

Entertainment Weekly reports the studio also offered her $4 million to make a sequel to The Lizzie McGuire Movie (she got $1 million for the first one) but the Duffs wanted more.

The Duffs and Disney each blame the other for the split. "We very much wanted to continue the Lizzie franchise," Disney Studio's Nina Jacobson told The Los Angeles Times. "But every deal has its tipping point, the point at which it no longer makes sense. Unfortunately, that's the point we reached in the Lizzie negotiations and we ultimately had to say goodbye."

"It's funny because I never, like, broke away," Hilary told Access Hollywood. "It wasn't like I'm leaving, I'm gone, I'm

Hils attends the premiere of The Lizzie McGuire Movie at the Tribeca Film Festival in New York City in May 2003.

what would you like to do?' And we just never had that with Disney."

Even after Hilary's very public break-up with Disney, fans continue to greet her by shouting: "It's Lizzie McGuire!"

"It doesn't really bother me that people call me that," she told The Associated Press, acknowledging that it probably will take some time before people begin to separate her from her TV namesake. After all, with 2.3 million viewers per episode, the show continues to be enormously popular.

So, is Hilary nervous about taking on new, more mature roles?

"Not at all," she told Fox News. "I'm always scared to do another TV show because Lizzie McGuire was such a hit, but I think I'll be Okay." ♥

done. It was never like that. All Disney Channel picks up their television shows for is 65 episodes. We did 65 episodes and we did The Lizzie McGuire Movie in Rome and it was exciting. But things just didn't work out for a second one."

Susan Duff added: "It was a situation where Hilary needed to step back and assess really what she wanted to do. We were in the wonderful position of having other networks call, take meetings with Hilary, see who she is and say 'What would you like to do? We'd like to do it with you,

Big Screen Dreams

Hilary's first role in a theatrical release, 1998's Playing by Heart, was so minor that her name didn't even appear in the credits. Discouraging? A little. But the movie gave Hilary a chance to learn from some truly talented performers, including Gena Rowlands, Sean Connery, Angelina Jolie, Ryan Phillippe, Gillian Anderson, Jon Stewart, Dennis Quaid, and Anthony Edwards.

Three years later, Hilary landed a role in Human Nature. The film didn't do well at the box

character as a child — and this time her name appeared on screen. It was a sign of bigger and better things to come.

The March 2003 release of Agent Cody Banks marked Hilary's first major theatrical production. The movie features Frankie Muniz as a typical teen who just happens to be a junior CIA agent. His training is put to the test when he's asked to pose as a prep school student and befriend the beautiful Natalie Connors (Hilary's character) in order to gain access to her scientist dad.

Casting Hilary in the film was Natalie Sellers' idea. Who's she? The 8-year-old daughter of producer Dylan Sellers.

"I told her about the movie," says Sellers, "and she said, 'You've just got to get Lizzie McGuire. Dad, she's perfect!'"

office, but it won rave reviews at the Sundance and Cannes film festivals. The story focuses on an obsessive scientist (Tim Robbins) and a female naturalist (Patricia Arquette) who discover a man born and raised in the wild. Hilary portrayed Arquette's

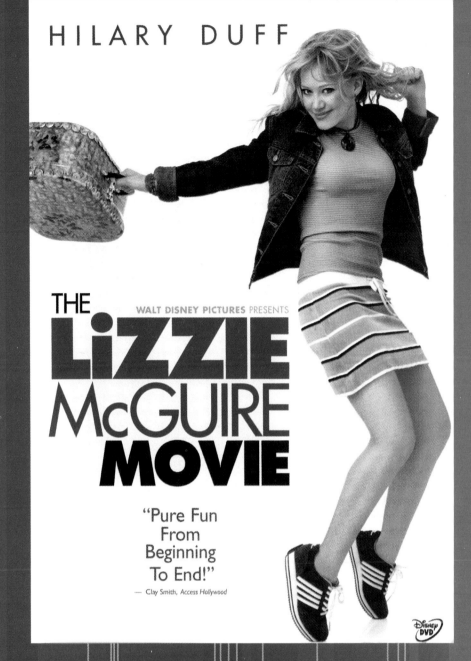

HILARY DUFF

WALT DISNEY PICTURES PRESENTS

THE LiZZiE McGUIRE MOVIE

"Pure Fun From Beginning To End!"
— Clay Smith, *Access Hollywood*

Not only did Sellers listen to his daughter, he also changed the name of the young heroine to Natalie to recognize her contribution.

Hilary first heard about Agent Cody Banks from her pal Frankie, when he was guest-starring on Lizzie McGuire. "Frankie was telling me about this really cool teenage spy action movie he was going to do," she says. "It sounded pretty exciting. Then my manager called about a week later and said there was a great part in this teenage James Bond movie and he thought I would be really cool in it. When I read the script, I just begged - please let me do it! I want to do it so much!"

Hilary says she was interested in the spy movie because it was so different from her TV show.

"The movie is crazy; it's action-packed," she told The New York Times Upfront.

"Every single day on the set, there were these big explosions. It was really cool to see how that worked, how they could put it together."

Hilary did some of her own stunt work for the movie but, because she didn't play a spy, she didn't have any big fight scenes.

Hilary says she's going to be picky. She wants parts that are differen

"But there is this one part where one of the bad guys kidnapped me," she told Upfront. "We ran outside and he was getting ready to throw me in a car and I climbed up the side of the car so he couldn't get me in there. It was really fun."

While Hilary enjoyed being part of the Agent Cody Banks film, starring in her own movie was a whole new experience.

Disney's 2003 The Lizzie McGuire Movie follows Lizzie and her pals – Gordo, Kate, and Ethan – on a class trip to Italy. Once there, Lizzie is mistaken for Isabella (who just happens to be an Italian pop star) and falls in love with Paolo (a handsome singer who just happens to be Isabella's former boyfriend). The plot required Hilary to play two characters: Lizzie and Isabella. It also gave her a chance to experiment with a different accent and hair color and, of course, wear the fabulous clothes Isabella likes to wear.

Part of The Lizzie McGuire Movie was filmed in Italy. Without hesitation Hilary says her favorite thing about the country was: Pizza!

"I ate pizza twice a day every day. It was amazing. And then I started going through pizza withdrawal when I went back to Vancouver (British Columbia, where the rest of the movie was filmed)."

While in Italy, the crew and cast were even allowed to film beside the Coliseum, a

about the movie roles she chooses.
from her Lizzie character.

Cheaper By The Dozen cast shot.

location that's generally off-limits to movie-makers.

"Using that location was a very sensitive issue for the Italians, but apparently this film was the first one in six years to be allowed to shoot outside the Coliseum. It was a wonderful honor," says director Jim Fall

With a successful TV show, a couple hit movies, and a chart-topping album to her credit, Hilary could have laid low for a while. Instead, she popped her career into turbo, filming two more movies – Cheaper by the Dozen and A Cinderella Story – in mid-2003.

Set for release Christmas 2003, Cheaper by the Dozen features Steve Martin as a successful small-town football coach and Bonnie Hunt as his wife. When dad gets an offer to coach a major college football team, they uproot their 12 children and move to the city where his increasing workload and his wife's book tour turn the kids' lives upside down. Hilary plays one of the children, along with stars Tom Welling, Piper Perabo, Jacob Smith, and Ashton Kutcher.

She says she decided to do the movie because she'd never been part of a large ensemble. Other pluses: the chance to work with Shawn Levy, a top-notch director, and an important story that shows the struggles of a family dealing with both happy and sad times.

Hilary scored $1 million for her role in Cheaper by the Dozen. She reportedly earned $2 million for A Cinderella Story in which she plays the part of Sam Martin, the Cinderella character. The movie, scheduled for release

"When you are working on a TV show everything goes really fast. You might do four scenes a day and then you do hair and makeup and then you have wardrobe fittings and then you go to school."

in July 2004, is a modern-day version of the classic fairytale, but instead of a horse and carriage, the prince drives a G55 Mercedes. The two meet in an Internet chat room, then again at a Halloween party. There's no glass slipper in this story. Instead, the young lovers are reunited thanks to Sam's lost cell phone.

Now that she's super experienced in both mediums, Hilary can honestly say that making a movie is much different than making a TV show.

"When you are working on a TV show everything goes really fast. You might do four scenes a day and then you do hair and makeup and then you have wardrobe fittings and then you go to school," she told Tribute's Bonnie Laufer. "Then when you do a movie it's slow, you might only do one or two scenes a day and there's a lot of sitting around and waiting. But I think that the product of a movie is better than TV."

Hilary obviously is drawn to

the big screen and producers know that movie-goers are drawn to her films. The Duffs now are sent hundreds of scripts each month but Hilary says she's going to be picky about the roles she chooses. She wants parts that are very different from her Lizzie character and she prefers mature roles that aren't too, uh, skanky.

The criteria are tough, but Hilary thinks she's found the next perfect part: the lead role in the upcoming The Perfect Man. The lighthearted Universal Pictures comedy is based on the lives of single mom Janet Robinson and her daughter, Heather. Hilary will play the Heather Robinson character.

With red-carpet premieres and awards shows, it's easy to see how Hilary could get caught up in all the glitz and glamour that goes along with being a movie star. She promises, though, that won't happen. She's too busy to get a big head – besides, she says, her family is always there to keep her humble. ♥

**Hilary attends
2003 MTV Movie Awards**
Photo by Robert Mora/Getty Images

31

Like pop superstars Britney, Justin, and Christina before her, Hilary has made the leap from the Disney Channel to MTV. And she's done it in a huge way!

Her rocking single "Why Not" – one of two songs she recorded for the Lizzie McGuire Movie Soundtrack – was a "Total Request Live" fave. And her first all-original, full-length album, Metamorphosis, soared to the top of the charts when it was released August 26, 2003.

Hils says two people influenced her decision to sing: her sister, Haylie, and on-again/off-again boyfriend Aaron Carter. When Aaron guest-starred on "Lizzie McGuire," Hilary watched him perform and thought, "I can do that." About the same time, she saw Haylie rehearsing with her band. They made singing and dancing look like so much fun, Hilary started taking lessons herself.

"I've always sung, ever since I could talk," says Hilary. "At home, at school, in the choir, everywhere. But about two years ago I decided to be a real singer, and started working with really cool singers, musicians and songwriters. Best of all, I started working in the studio, experimenting and putting material together. I've really fallen in love with the studio."

Hilary says the transition to singing wasn't as difficult as you might imagine. She was already in the Disney family because of Lizzie, so Buena Vista Records took her on and she didn't have to send out demo tapes like most other new musicians do.

She got her start recording songs for the Lizzie television and movie soundtracks. With her character Lizzie pretending to be Italian pop star Isabella, Hilary got a chance to sing in 2003's The Lizzie McGuire Movie. She was star-struck when she found herself among acts including Atomic Kitten, Vitamin C, the Beu Sisters, and even the late Dean Martin on the flick's soundtrack.

The CD, from Walt Disney Records, features Hilary singing two songs: "What Dreams Are Made Of" and "Why Not." Both singles became smash hits on Radio Disney.

Hils was honored to have a song - "The Tiki, Tiki,

Hilary hugs singer Aaron Carter as they attend the premiere of The Lizzie McGuire Movie in Hollywood.

Hilary attends Nickelodeon's 16th Annual Kid's Choice Awards in Santa Monica, California.

Photo by Frank Micelotta/Getty Images

Tiki Room" – included on Disneymania. The album featured singles by Anastasia, Ashanti, Smash Mouth, Usher, and others and quickly became gold-certified, selling more than 500,000 copies.

In October 2002 she released a special Christmas album - Santa Claus Lane – and then, 10 months later, fans got to hear her pop album, Metamorphosis, for the first time.

Hilary didn't write any of the songs on Metamorphosis, but Haylie did ("Sweet Sixteen" and "Inner Strength"). Hilary was thrilled to be able to bring her sister's lyrics to life. She also was excited to collaborate with the Matrix, who have worked with Avril Lavigne, Christina Aguilera, and Liz Phair, and with William Orbit who produced Ray of Light for Madonna.

After years of being overshadowed by Lizzie's TV personality, Hilary was grateful for the chance to record songs that reflect her true identity with themes ranging from friendship and girl power to being ignored by boyfriends and running in the sun. She chose the album's title because she was at a place in her life where everything was changing.

Metamorphosis is heavily inspired by Hilary's own music collection: Britney Spears, Michelle Branch, and Vanessa Carlton. Her wide-ranging musical tastes also are inspired by Janis Joplin, Bob Dylan, Sublime, 50 Cent, For Soup, No Doubt and Good Charlotte, Linkin Park, and Boomkat.

Clearly, her fans appreciate the changes Hilary has gone through. The single "So Yesterday" captured the top spot on

Billboard's Hot 100 Singles Sales chart and made waves at Top 40 radio – including New York's Z100, where it became the station's most-requested song.

"So Yesterday" also was a smash on TV and online. MTV hosted a premiere party for the "So Yesterday" music video. Thanks to fans' calls, Hilary's video zoomed up the "TRL" countdown to become the show's No. 2 request. "So Yesterday," filmed on Venice Beach in Los Angeles, also was the most-streamed video on AOL.

Metamorphosis sold 204,000 copies in the United States during its first week. Hilary has traveled extensively to promote the CD, making personal appearances at malls and music stores in cities including New York, Miami, Denver, and Toronto. She also did her first live shows during a fall 2003 U.S. concert tour.

Even with all her success, Hilary admits she's done what nearly every other girl has: practiced singing in front of her mirror into brushes and hairdryers!

Haylie is featured on Hilary's holiday song "Same Old Christmas," but they have yet to record a pop duet together. "We haven't found the right song," explains Hilary. In the meantime, she appreciates Haylie's awesome songwriting talents.

"I have a song called 'I Need a Sunday' that my sister wrote for me," she told MTV. "And it's totally relating to my life, about how it's just crazy and hectic and busy and how I just need some time to breathe."

With TV guest appearances, an album to promote, fans to meet, and major motion pictures to complete, it's certain Hilary's life will be crazy, hectic and busy for some time to come. ♥

FANS LOVE HILARY

because kids mobbed her. These days Hilary can't go anywhere without being swarmed by fans. Malls have had to be closed

A male fan showed up at MTV Studios in April 2003, when Hilary was hosting TRL, wearing a costume that looked like a giant bun. Hilary told People magazine about the incident, recalling that he held a sign that said: "I dressed up as a hot dog for you. I'm a dork."

He was among 4,000 or so fans hoping for a glimpse of the young star. Some traveled hundreds of miles and stood in line beginning at 3 in the morning.

A month later, Hilary's appearance at Manhattan's Disney Store attracted such a huge throng of fans that traffic on nearby Fifth Avenue came to a standstill.

In September 2003, more than 1,000 young girls and their parents paid $100 per person to attend a celebrity challenge event Hilary hosted in Toronto. Earlier that day, a lucky 100 kids got to attend high tea with Hilary – at $5,000 a piece. The events benefited a variety of children's charities.

Hilary's management reports that her web site (www.hilaryduff.com) pulls in more than 300,000 fan letters a week. And there are dozens of fan web sites dedicated to the spunky Texas teen.

No doubt about it: Hilary Duff is red hot.

The young actress struggled for so many years to land even the tiniest of parts that she was unprepared for the huge fan reaction that came with Lizzie McGuire's success.

"I kind of expected it, but I didn't think it would be so big, especially when the show first came out," she told PBSkids.org. "At first a couple of people would recognize me here and there. Now, going to restaurants is hard or going to the mall is hard."

"It's very cool though," she added. "It's nice to know that people like the show and they like what you're doing. It gives you a feeling of accomplishment."

A lot of Hilary's friends are in the business, so they understand the complications that come with being a celebrity. Still, sneaking out for a bite with buddies isn't easy.

"When we go out to dinner, there's this restaurant called Bob's Big Boy which is by my house and it's open all night, so we go really late," Hilary told Your Magazine. "Even then, it's hard because people will form a line down the restaurant to my table and the restaurant won't do anything about it, so my friends will finally say, 'She's eating right now. Will you leave us alone?' It's kind of hard."

"It's nice to know that people like the show and they like what you're doing."

"I'm used to it," she says. "So, I'm always really nice to people and sometimes I'll say, 'Oh, I'm just hanging out with my friends being normal right now, so thanks for watching the show' or something. Usually I'll sign autographs (and) take pictures. It's so much easier to be nice to them than it is to be rude."

Life in the public eye isn't easy, but you won't hear Hilary complain. She only hopes fans aren't watching with a super-critical eye. "There are times it's hard because sometimes you feel like going to get something to eat and just want to feed your face but you can't always do that," she told

Hils accepts her award as the Movie Breakout Actress for The Lizzie McGuire Movie at the 2003 Teen Choice Awards in Universal City, California.

"Usually I'll sign autographs (and)
to be nice to (fans) thar

fans during an online chat in August 2003.

In fact, Hilary made national headlines in September 2003 when she criticized fellow pop star Avril Lavigne. It seems Avril had dissed her own fans for copying her style and wearing ties over tank tops.

In one interview Avril said: "I sometimes see girls who are dressed like me and made-up like me. Get a life, you know."

That kind of talk incensed Hilary who believes performers should respect their admirers.

"I think some of the things Avril said about her fans were kind of mean-spirited," Hilary told Teenhollywood.com. "I was like, 'You should be happy these people like you and look up to you.'"

Of course, some meetings with fans are odder than others. Hilary told The New York Post in March 2003 that one of her strangest encounters took place at Bloomingdale's department store.

"This girl who was my age was following me around the store for 10 minutes. Finally I looked at her and I said 'Hi,' and she ran away," recalls Hilary. "So her mom came up to me and was like, 'Are you that girl from Lizzie McGuire?' And the girl slapped her mom on the arm. Then the mom pushed the girl and the girl pulled the mom's hair. And I had not said anything. Then the girl ran off and the mom looks at me and said, 'Thanks a lot – you just embarrassed my daughter.' I was like: 'I'm sorry.'"

Being a role model isn't easy, but Hilary is happy to have fans look up to her. She says she looked up to people when she was growing up – including boy

ake pictures. It's so much easier
t is to be rude."

group Hanson and actor Jonathon Taylor Thomas.

"People are always saying 'do you feel a responsibility because so many people look up to you' but not really," she told A Girls World in March 2003. I think it's really cool that they like me or my show. Also I think maybe kids should look up to people that have changed the world, like doctors or astronauts or something like that. So it feels kind of weird but it's nice to know that they like me and look up to me."

Of course, along with the fans, Hilary has had to learn to deal with more than her share of gossip. Ever since word got out that she dated singer Aaron Carter, she's been the subject of some very mean-spirited Internet posts. There have been rumors about her drinking, doing drugs, sleeping with co-stars, and having her breasts enlarged. How does she deal with it?

"I just let it slide off my back," she tells Bopmag.com.

Hilary has even had a suspected stalker. A man had been sitting in his parked car outside the Duff's Toluca Lake home for several hours on August 5, 2003, when big sis Haylie saw the car. Hilary's mom jumped in her car and chased him for 50 minutes through the California suburb.

Sure, popularity has its downsides: lack of privacy, being the subject of gossip, and being unable to do simple things like go to the mall or a movie. Still, Hilary wouldn't give it up for anything.

"It makes it really hard to go out," she told MTV. "But it's cool at the same time because these are the people that let me do what I love to do every single day."

47

BRITNEY

Photo by Frederick M. Brown/Getty Images

HILARY

49

Name
Britney
Jean Spears

Born
Dec. 2, 1981

Sign
Sagittarius

Eye Color
Brown

Hometown
Kentwood,
Louisiana

Nicknames
Bit-Bit, Brit

Parents
Jamie and
Lynne Spears

Siblings
Bryan and
Jamie Lynn

Pastime
Shopping

Big Break
"Mickey
Mouse Club"

Debut Single
"Baby
One More Time"

Started as
State champion
gymnast

Is Hilary posed to become the next BIG thing? Will she fill Britney's shoes as the queen of MTV? Will she shed her virtuous image for the sake of selling CDs? Those are questions entertainment writers and trend-watchers around the world are asking – and answering.

Zac Crain, music editor at the Dallas Observer says comparing Hilary to Britney would be "kind of like comparing apples and ... apple pie" (Hilary's the apple pie).

He says Hilary's managers and agents have done well, moving her from TV to movies to music — and succeeding at all three.

"She might even be on track to becoming bigger than Britney because she has a built-in audience who will buy whatever she's selling," Crain says. "Not to mention that she's already got a hit with her Lizzie McGuire movie, something that couldn't be said for (Britney's movie) Crossroads."

Maggie Dumais, senior vice president of licensing for Bravado International Group (the company behind "Stuff by Hilary Duff"), is quick to say: "No, Hilary Duff is not becoming the next Britney. She is a complete original."

Both young stars, says Dumais, are very talented and beautiful, but they have distinct styles. She says Hilary's new fashion line is an age-appropriate, fashion-forward line for tweens and teens. Britney leans toward more mature — and often more-revealing — fashions.

One thing's for sure. Hilary is going to have to grow up in public, just as Britney, Melissa Joan Hart, and Mary-Kate and Ashley Olsen have before her.

When Britney, for example, wore hot pants for a Rolling Stone cover shot, she faced a lot of criticism. The suggestive photo got tongues wagging and prompted the media watchdog group American Family Association to start a Britney boycott.

Britney defended her decision in her 2001

51

Hilary at a Glance

Name
Hilary Ann Duff

Born
Sept. 28, 1987

Sign
Libra

Eye Color
Hazel

Hometown
Houston, Texas

Nicknames
Hils, Juicy

Parents
Bob and
Susan Duff

Siblings
Haylie

Pets
Two dogs:
Little Dog and
Remington

Pastime
Shopping

Big Break
"Casper
Meets Wendy"

Debut Single
"I Can't Wait"

Started as
Six-year-old
ballerina

"I love Britney Spears. She's awesome
CDs and I know all the words t

biography Britney Spears by Sarah Delmage: "I was becoming a young woman. It's nice to feel sexy sometimes."

Similarly, Melissa Joan Hart, who started acting when she was just 3, got in trouble with Sabrina producers when she posed in revealing outfits on two magazine covers. She says growing up on screen is weird at first. "Then you become more comfortable — but you never really get used to it."

Crain says dealing with her emerging sexuality likely will be a challenge for Hilary, too. "She's got the same virginal image Britney used to have — even more so. That'll be tough to shake."

As for Hilary, she's happy for the comparison to one of her longtime idols. When Entertainment Weekly asked her if she wanted to be as big as Britney, the Texas teen replied: "Britney Spears? That sounds so huge! She's awesome, I love her so much. And I think it's been really hard for her – like all the things you see her go through in the press and stuff. But I would love for my albums to be as successful as hers have been."

When Hilary appeared on MTV's Total Request Live in August 2003, she responded to a report that Britney had complimented her "amazing" music and how she was "completely a light to the world so beautiful, so incredibly sweet." Said Hilary: "Oh, that makes me feel so good, you guys. I love Britney Spears. She's awesome. I'm a huge fan . . . I have all of her CDs and I know all the words to her songs. I think she gets a lot of flak and stuff and I love her. She is awesome."

No doubt about it, Britney Spears has grown up. She's no longer the perky schoolgirl she used to be. For now, much of Hilary's appeal is that she does come off as a blonde and dimpled, real-deal teenager. She's chirpy and trendy without being trashy. She actually blushed when she was nominated as "Best Female Hottie" at the 2003 Teen Choice Awards.

So, now that Britney has become the Queen of Rock, will Hilary be crowned Princess of Pop? Only time will tell. ♥

m a huge fan . . . I have all of her
er songs. She is awesome."

What's Next? for Hilary

What's Next for Hilary?

In Fall 2003, Hilary landed on the cover of Vanity Fair magazine along with Mary-Kate and Ashley Olson, Amanda Bynes and others, as one of the 20 "Hot Teens" in Hollywood.

"Young girls are taking roles that are older to prove their breadth of acting. With Hilary, to be able to get appropriate roles and to have studios that are right – that's the challenge."

"Hot" might be an understatement. Hilary is on fire and she doesn't show signs of burning out anytime soon. In fact, with success in TV, music, and movies, she's well on her way to becoming a superstar!

Of course, superstardom brings its own new challenges.

"Young actors face the problem of whether they can be adults, without necessarily taking that step too early in their career," Disney Channel Entertainment President Rich Ross told New York Daily News. "Young girls are taking roles that are older to prove their breadth of acting. With Hilary, to be able to get appropriate roles and to have studios that are right – that's the challenge."

56

Hilary attends the premiere of The Lizzie McGuire Movie in Hollywood.

Photo by Lucy Nicholson/Getty Images

57

What's Next for Hilary?

Hilary knows it won't be easy. "I have to pick projects that don't talk down to the younger audience because they're definitely important, but that can also expand the audience into older kids," she told MTV.com. She's confident her future is bright. After all, she has her family to help navigate the rough waters.

"If I didn't have people around me telling me smart choices to make, then I definitely wouldn't be where I am right now," she said. "I definitely make decisions for myself, though. I have to follow what I feel is right for me. You just have to make sure you always pick great projects."

In addition to performing, Hilary is becoming a true marketing powerhouse, especially with teens and tweens.

In July 2003, Hilary kicked off a major marketing campaign for Hasbro's VideoNow, a take-along video player. Hilary appears in commercials for the gadget and stars in a special disc, A Day in the Life of Hilary Duff, made for the video promotion.

"I have to pick projects that don't talk down to the younger audience because they're definitely important, but that can also expand the audience into older kids."

Hilary poses backstage with Amanda Bynes (of The Amanda Show) at The 2003 MTV Movie Awards.

Photo by Kevin Winter/Getty Images

59

What's Next for Hilary?

Visa has introduced a Hilary Duff prepaid credit card especially for teens.

And Hilary's "Stuff by Duff" line of cosmetics is due out in Fall 2003, followed by apparel, cosmetics, fashion dolls, footwear, jewelry, underwear, and pet products in Spring 2004. The company that's licensing the products says the line will stick around long after Hilary is past her teens. Company executives predict sales of the merchandise could exceed hundreds of millions of dollars.

Hilary told Extra that the new clothing line is important to her because: "I want to get the message out there that you can dress cool and it can be edgy without having to show off your boobs, your butt, you know."

Packaging for the makeup will be recyclable and the star has picked out a range of pinks that should suit all complexions. Another reason to adore Hilary – all the makeup items will be priced under $4.

"It's weird that my name would be on something and make someone want to buy it," Hilary told USA Today. "It's crazy because I'm such a normal teenager." ♥

It's weird that my name would be on something and make someone want to buy it. It's crazy because I'm such a normal teenager."

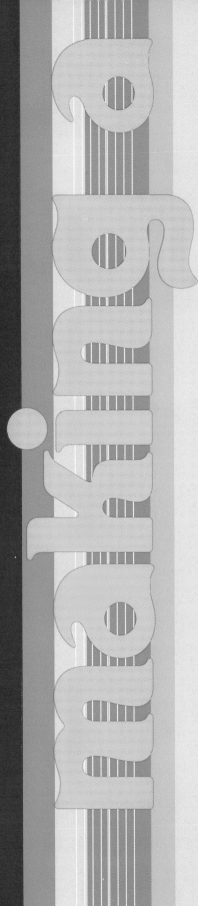

Hilary Duff makes a big splash on stage and, thanks to her volunteer work, she's also making a big difference in communities across the country.

Hilary has worked with dozens of organizations – like Colorado Kids and Kids with a Cause — to reward volunteerism and get other teens active in giving back to their neighborhoods. She regularly visits children in hospitals to help make their days a little brighter and escorts disadvantaged youth to theme parks and shares in the fun and the thrill of the rides.

Spending time with less fortunate children is very important to Hilary. She has been super active in Kids With a Cause since the group began in 1999. The organization was created to provide a helping hand to the children of world who, through no fault of their own, suffer from poverty, hunger, sickness, lack of education, abandonment, neglect, or abuse. The 80-plus members behind Kids With a Cause are mostly celebrities from film, TV and the recording industry who

Lizzie McGuire co-star Lalaine Veraga-Paras and Hilary volunteer to refurbish the grounds at the Boys and Girls Club of Burbank in Burbank, CA.

Photo by Robert Mora/Getty Images

63

realize they have been very fortunate and who want to donate their time to help others. Other famous members include Chioke (MTV Duets), Michael Welch (Joan of Arcadia), Jacquie Willey (Even Stevens), and Hilary's sister Haylie.

In September 2003, Hilary went to Toronto to help start the Canadian chapter of Kids With a Cause. Zellers department stores even made a $10,000 donation to the charity as a 16th birthday present to Hilary.

"We're trying to get kids around the United States to get out there and volunteer," she says. "Most kids think that they're only one person but they really can do a lot."

Hilary credits her parents for igniting her volunteer spirit.

She told PBSKids.org: "My mom is into charity. If we have a dinner party or a birthday party, she tells people, 'Don't bring presents for us, bring diapers or something so we can give it away.' I think the influence from my parents started it for me and my sister.

It's really important to give back."

Hilary has served on the Advisory Board of the Audrey Hepburn Child Benefit Fund. The non-profit organization was started in 1994 to further actress Audrey Hepburn's international appeals on behalf of suffering children around the world. Hepburn died in 1993. The charity now is based in Los Angeles and works to:

• Educate children in Somalia, Sudan, Eritrea, Ethiopia, and Rwanda.

• Provide medical and mental health treatment to abused children in a "child friendly" environment.

• Work with the U.S. Fund for UNICEF to bring 120 million children worldwide back to school.

• Fight sexual exploitation of children in Central America.

Hilary loves animals and also enjoys working with charities that benefit them. Her Fox Terrier/Chihuahua mix Little Dog has become so popular that a line of dog clothing called "Little Dog Duff" is being designed and sold to benefit Utah's Best Friends animal sanctuary. Best Friends works with humane organizations and people all across the nation who want to be sure every healthy dog and cat has a good home with a loving family.

In July 2003, Hilary went to California's Return to Freedom Ranch for a photo shoot for an upcoming book about

Hilary also has begun working with Angelwear, an organization that raises funds and awareness for non-profit groups. The superstar has designed her own artwork for Angelwear that's being produced on tees and tanks. Sales of the clothing benefit Kids With a Cause and Ocean

"We're trying to get kids around the United States to get out there and volunteer. Most kids think that they're only one person but they really can do a lot."

celebrities and horses. While there, Hilary had the opportunity to tour the animal sanctuary and learn more about Return to Freedom's goal of saving the American Wild Horse. When she was asked if she would become Return to Freedom's Official Youth Ambassador, she said she would be honored.

Raised on a ranch near Houston, Hilary said: "I love horses, and I love being out here. This so reminds me of home."

of Love, an organization that helps children with cancer and their families.

Hosting celebrity challenges, concerts, and even tea parties has allowed Hilary to raise hundreds of thousands of dollars for charities around the world.

And no matter how famous she becomes, Hilary says she'll always make time in her schedule to volunteer. She knows how lucky she is in life, and she's dedicated to helping those less fortunate. ♥

Hilary
STUFF

Q&A with America's Number One Teen Queen Hilary Duff

Hilary has quickly become one of the hottest young TV, film and recording stars. But what makes her tick? What does she do when she's not glamming it up on the red carpet?

She loves to spend time with her family, friends, and her two dogs, Remington and Little Dog. She likes to talk about boys, shop, and try out makeup tricks with her pal Taylor.

Hils also loves to talk with fans. She makes lots of appearances, enjoys meeting fans after her concerts, and keeps a diary on her website. She says it's mind-boggling that 5,000 fans will show up at a mall when she's there to sign autographs, and she often stays hours longer than scheduled so she can meet as many people as possible.

"These people are the people that let me do what I love to do every single day," she told MTV.com.

Here she shares with fans her thoughts on everything from music and books to dating and school:

Q. What do you like to read?

A. Chicken Soup for the Soul books. I'll be reading one of those and I'll either laugh hysterically or start bawling. I love Harry Potter books and I love all the movies, too. When I was young, I really was into Shel Silverstein books. I used to memorize them and stuff like that. And also I read a book the other day, Holes. It's about these delinquent boys who go to camp. But it is an amazing story.

Q. What do you do in your free time?

A. I play The Sims game on my laptop. I got totally hooked on it and now I'm getting everybody around me hooked on it as well.

Q. You've been doing commercials for everything from milk to video players. Is there anything else you'd like to promote?

A. Dr. Pepper. I drink it all the time. It's always on my sets.

Q. What's it like to watch yourself on TV?

A. It is really weird. I am my own worst critic, so if I do something I am like, Oh why did I do that?

Q. Are you like Lizzie?

A. Lizzie is not really comfortable in her own skin – she is kind of shy. I'm pretty shy, but I can be outgoing also. Lizzie really can't. We're also different in that she goes to a regular school and she doesn't have many friends. She is just trying to find herself.

Q. What's dating like when you're a celebrity?

A. I never want to date anyone in the business again because of the whole thing with Aaron Carter. It's just a big mess. And it's hard for me to meet normal guys because I'm always working and I don't go to regular school. And if I did, they wouldn't understand why I go out of town so much. I think I'm going to have to wait till I'm older.

Q. If you could work with any singer or actor who would it be?

A. That's a hard question because I like so many different people. I'd like to work with Sandra Bullock because she's funny, pretty, and a great actress.

Q. If you weren't a celebrity, what do you think you'd be doing?

A. I always wanted to be a veterinarian when I was younger but then I figured out that animals actually die there, so that was not the job for me. Definitely something with kids or animals or something like that.

Q. When you were younger, did you dream of becoming a star?

A.   When I was a little girl, I didn't think this is what I wanted to do. My older sister actually wanted to be an actress and singer and, of course being the younger sister, I wanted to do everything she did. Then I started loving acting classes and we talked my mom into taking us to California. Then we went on many, many auditions until I got Lizzie McGuire.

Q. What is your favorite movie?

A.   There are a lot of different movies I like from different genres. I like I am Sam, Drop Dead Gorgeous and Chicago.

Q. Do you do your own hair?

A.   A lot of times I go to events I do my own hair and makeup because I like to do that stuff. But I do work with a hair and makeup stylist because I like to learn new tricks. Whenever I work I use a stylist. It's fun to find someone you can give input to.

Q. What was it like recording your first album?

A.   It was hard because you have to pick material you really love because you have to sing it all the time. In the studio there may be songs harder to sing than others, but I enjoyed being in the studio because I got to work with a lot of great people. I enjoy seeing what other people's work ethic is, how much they put into a song. It was a really fun experience.

"You have to let rumors roll off you
Girls who go around school

Q. What do you like to listen to?

A. I listen to everything. I like the Eagles, Bob Dylan and Janis Joplin. I also like 50 Cent, Black Eyed Peas, Justin Timberlake, Britney Spears, and Vanessa Carlton.

Q. Your fans adore you.
Do you ever wish they'd just go away?

A. It definitely makes it really hard to go shopping or to the movies or – I mean, it makes it really hard to go out. But it's really cool at the same time because these are the people that let me do what I love to do every single day. It does get hard sometimes but it's nice and it's rewarding.

Q. How do you handle hearing rumors about yourself or reading stories in the tabloids that aren't true?

A. You have to let rumors roll off your back, even in everyday life. Girls who go around school gossiping – half the stuff's not true. You have to keep telling yourself that.

back, even in everyday life.
ossiping – half the stuff's not true."

Q. How has fame changed your life?

A. People think it is so different from regular life and I don't think it is at all. I just go do my job. After work, I go home and do my chores and I make my bed and I do my homework. So, it is just kind of like a sport to me. All my friends play sports and I work on a TV show.

Q. Any advice for kids seeking the kind of fame you've already attained?

A. Don't do it for the fame. This life can be kind of nuts sometimes.

Q. Do you see yourself as a role model?

A. I get fan mail that says, "You're my role model, I'm your biggest fan. I look up to you." It makes me feel really good, but I'm not saving lives here. I love acting, I love what I do, but kids should be looking up to people like doctors or scientists or presidents that have changed the world in some way. But it does feel good to know that someone might look up to me.

Q. Do you have any deep, dark secrets?

A. I have glasses. I thought glasses were cool for a while, so I have some because one eye can't see as well as the other. They're cute. I wear them sometimes, like to the mall. I also think I'm going to get Invisialign (braces) because my teeth are messed up.

HILLARY DUFF
Movie, Music and Television Credits

Movie Releases

The Perfect Man
(Universal Pictures) TBA
Role: Heather Robinson character

Cinderella
(Warner Brothers) 2004
Role: Sam Martin

Cheaper by the Dozen
(20th Century Fox) 2003
Role: Lorraine Baker

The Lizzie McGuire Movie
(Walt Disney Pictures) 2003
Role: Lizzie McGuire

Agent Cody Banks
(MGM) 2003
Role: Natalie Connors

Human Nature
(Fine Line Features) 2001
Role: Young Lila Jute

Playing by Heart
(Miramax Films) 1998
Role: Uncredited

Video

Lizzie McGuire: Fashionably Lizzie
(Buena Vista Home Entertainment) 2002
Role: Lizzie McGuire

Lizzie McGuire: Growing Up Lizzie
(Buena Vista Home Entertainment) 2002
Role: Lizzie McGuire

Casper Meets Wendy
(20th Century Fox / SabanEntertainment) 1998
Role: Wendy

Television

Lizzie McGuire
(Disney) 2001-2004
Role: Lizzie McGuire

Cadet Kelly
(Disney) 2002
Role: Kelly Collins

The George Lopez Show
(Warner Bros. Television) 2002
Role: Cosmetics salesperson

Chicago Hope
(20th Century Fox Television) 2000
Role: Jessie Seldon

The Soul Collector
(Hearst Entertainment/Brayton-Carlucci Productions) 1999
Role: Ellie

True Women
(Hallmark Entertainment) 1997
Role: Child Number 1

"He's so cute!
He's cool. He's
very attractive but
he's nice, too. He's
very cool."

HILARY DUFF
about Ashton Kutcher,
That '70s Show,
Punk'd,
and *Cheaper*
by the Dozen.

"If you meet my
mom and you really
know my mom and you
know our family, she is
the nicest woman ever.
She's smart. She's not
going to let anybody
take advantage or
let anything bad
happen."

HILARY DUFF
about her mom.

"I'm a totally
normal kid. When
I come home I have
to take the trash
out and feed
my dog and make
my bed."

HILARY DUFF

"Duff is a true beauty with a dazzling smile and pop stardom is already hers."

ROGER EBERT,
Chicago Sun-Times
movie critic.

"Hilary made a record that will reach her fan base and beyond, marking her 'metamorphosis' from a TV and movie star to a full-fledged musical artist."

BOB CAVALLO
Buena Vista Music
Group Chairman

"She's definitely not Britney, by any means, but she's quickly moving up the ranks."

JEN SMITH
Teen People editor

HILLARY DUFF
Movie, Music and Television Credits

Music

Metamorphosis
(Buena Vista Records) 8/2003
"So Yesterday"
"Come Clean"
"Workin' It Out"
"Little Voice"
"Where Did I Go Right?"
"Anywhere But Here"
"The Math"
"Love Just Is"
"Sweet Sixteen"
"Party Up"
"Metamorphosis"
"Inner Strength"
"Why Not"

The Lizzie McGuire Soundtrack
(Disney) 4/2003
"Why Not?"
"What Dreams are Made Of"
"Why Not McMix"

Santa Clause 2 Soundtrack
(Disney) 11/2002
"Santa Claus Lane"

Santa Claus Lane
(Disney) 10/2002
"Santa Claus Lane"
"Santa Claus is Coming to Town"
"I Heard Santa on the Radio"
(with Christina Milian)
"Jingle Bell Rock"
"Sleigh Ride"
"Tell Me a Story" (with Lil' Romeo)
"Last Christmas"
"Same Old Christmas" (with Haylie Duff)
"Wonderful Christmas Time"

Disneymania
(Disney) 9/2002
"The Tiki, Tiki, Tiki Room"

Lizzie McGuire Soundtrack
(Buena Vista Records) 8/2002
"I Can't Wait"

Test Yourself
Think You Know Your Duff Stuff?

You've participated in her live online chats. You bought Metamorphosis the day it was released. And you've never missed an episode of *Lizzie McGuire*. You think you know everything about Hilary Duff ... but do you? Put your knowledge to the test with these ten questions.

1. Which star did not do a guest appearance on *Lizzie McGuire*?

a) Steven Tyler, lead singer of *Aerosmith*

b) Doris Roberts, star of *Everybody Loves Raymond*

c) Courtney Cox, star of *Friends*

d) Frankie Muniz, star of *Malcolm in the Middle*

2. Hilary's dad is:

a) an attorney

b) a veterinarian

c) partner in a chain of convenience stores

d) a high-tech exec

3. The WB Network celebrated Hilary's 16th birthday by airing her taped concert performances from:

a) Hawaii

b) Rome

c) Spain

d) New York City

4. Hilary's 2002 holiday CD includes duets with these two artists:

a) Lil' Romeo and Christina Milian

b) Nelly and P. Diddy

c) Christina Aguilera and Lil' Kim

d) Michelle Branch and Ashanti

5. Hilary shares her September 28 birthday with:

a) Gwyneth Paltrow

b) Cameron Diaz

c) Naomi Campbell

d) Mandy Moore

6. What school does Hilary's Lizzie McGuire character attend?

a) Jason Lee Middle School

b) Lambert Middle School

c) Hillridge Middle School

d) Washington Middle School

7. What sport is Hilary crazy about?

a) Soccer

b) Volleyball

c) Gymnastics

d) Cycling

8. What are Hilary's favorite subjects in school?

a) English and social studies

b) History and math

c) P.E. and word processing

d) Creative writing and biology

9. *Lizzie McGuire* premiered in what year?

a) 1999

b) 2000

c) 2001

d) 2002

10. Which of Hilary's songs includes the lyrics "my blonde hair is everywhere"?

a) "Sweet Sixteen"

b) "Yesterday"

c) "Party Up"

d) "Why Not"

Check your score:

Give yourself one point for each correct answer.

10 correct:
Are you related to Hilary? You really know your stuff!

8-9 correct:
Good enough. You're tough on Duff stuff!

6-7 correct:
Were you doing homework when you should have been watching Lizzie McGuire?

5 or fewer correct:
Go straight to the video store and rent *Human Nature*, *Agent Cody Banks* and *The Lizzie McGuire Movie*. Afterward, pop Metamorphosis into your CD player and listen to it three times. Then, take the test again!

Answers: Hold this page in front of a mirror to read the answers.

(1) c. Courtney Cox never made a guest appearance in this slate. (2) c. He co-owns a chain of convenience stores. (3) a. The show was taped on the island of Maui. (4) a. Lil' Romeo and Christina Milian (5) b. Cameron Diaz and Hilary share her birthday with Gwyneth Paltrow (6) c. She calls Hillridge Middle School through the day. (7) c. She attends Hillridge Middle School. (8) b. She likes math history and word processing. (9) a. The Lizzie McGuire Movie in 2001 and will air new episodes into 2004. (10) a. "Sweet Sixteen's" lyrics are "Blue skies are above me, am I, you who love me, and "My blonde hair is everywhere."

80